EMMANUEL JOSEPH

The Marketplace of Ideas, How Politics and Society Shape Global Business

Copyright © 2025 by Emmanuel Joseph

All rights reserved. No part of this publication may be reproduced, stored or transmitted in any form or by any means, electronic, mechanical, photocopying, recording, scanning, or otherwise without written permission from the publisher. It is illegal to copy this book, post it to a website, or distribute it by any other means without permission.

First edition

This book was professionally typeset on Reedsy.
Find out more at reedsy.com

Contents

1	Chapter 1: The Interplay of Politics and Business	1
2	Chapter 2: The Evolution of Global Trade Policies	3
3	Chapter 3: The Role of Government Regulations	6
4	Chapter 4: Political Risk and Business Strategy	9
5	Chapter 5: Societal Values and Corporate Responsibility	12
6	Chapter 6: The Influence of Political Lobbying	15
7	Chapter 7: The Impact of Geopolitical Conflicts	17
8	Chapter 8: The Role of International Organizations	20
9	Chapter 9: The Power of Public Opinion	23
10	Chapter 10: The Challenges of Global Governance	26
11	Chapter 11: The Future of Work in a Changing World	30
12	Chapter 12: Navigating the Marketplace of Ideas	33

1

Chapter 1: The Interplay of Politics and Business

The complex relationship between politics and business has shaped the global economy throughout history. Political systems and ideologies dictate the rules of the marketplace, influence trade policies, and affect business practices. In democratic societies, businesses must navigate the intricacies of government regulations, lobbying efforts, and political campaigns. Conversely, authoritarian regimes impose strict controls and centralized decision-making, leading to different economic outcomes. Understanding these dynamics is essential for businesses operating in diverse political landscapes. This chapter delves into historical examples and contemporary scenarios where politics and business intersect.

One of the most illustrative examples of the interplay between politics and business is the case of the East India Company. Established in the 17th century, this British trading corporation had significant influence over political affairs in India. Through its monopolistic trade practices and the support of the British Crown, the East India Company effectively governed large parts of India, demonstrating how business interests can shape political power. This historical case underscores the potential for business entities to wield political influence, often blurring the lines between commercial and governmental roles.

THE MARKETPLACE OF IDEAS, HOW POLITICS AND SOCIETY SHAPE GLOBAL BUSINESS

In contemporary times, the influence of politics on business is evident in various regions. In the United States, the relationship between the federal government and major corporations is characterized by lobbying efforts and regulatory negotiations. Tech giants like Google, Amazon, and Facebook engage in extensive lobbying to shape policies related to data privacy, antitrust regulations, and digital commerce. These efforts highlight the strategic importance of political engagement for businesses seeking to navigate complex regulatory environments and protect their interests.

On the other hand, in authoritarian regimes, the interplay between politics and business takes a different form. In countries like China, the government exerts significant control over the economy, with state-owned enterprises playing a dominant role. The Chinese Communist Party's influence extends to major private companies, which are often required to align their business practices with the party's objectives. This centralized approach to economic governance creates a unique business environment where political directives shape corporate strategies and market dynamics.

Understanding these dynamics is crucial for businesses operating in diverse political landscapes. Companies must develop strategies to engage with political stakeholders, adapt to regulatory changes, and navigate the risks associated with political instability. By examining historical and contemporary examples, this chapter provides insights into the intricate relationship between politics and business, offering valuable lessons for companies operating in the global marketplace.

2

Chapter 2: The Evolution of Global Trade Policies

Global trade policies have undergone significant transformations over the centuries, influenced by political agendas and societal needs. From the mercantilist practices of the 16th century to the liberalization trends of the 20th century, trade policies have been a reflection of the prevailing political ideologies. This chapter explores the evolution of trade agreements, tariffs, and protectionist measures, examining their impact on global business operations. By analyzing key milestones such as the establishment of the World Trade Organization (WTO) and the rise of regional trade blocs, we gain insights into how politics shape the rules of international trade.

The 16th and 17th centuries were dominated by mercantilist policies, where nations sought to amass wealth through a favorable balance of trade. Countries imposed high tariffs and restrictive trade policies to protect their domestic industries and accumulate precious metals. This era was marked by intense competition among European powers for colonial dominance, with trade monopolies and state-sponsored enterprises playing pivotal roles in economic expansion. The mercantilist approach laid the foundation for the global trade network, shaping the dynamics of international commerce for centuries to come.

The 19th century saw a shift towards trade liberalization, driven by the principles of free trade and economic interdependence. The British Corn Laws, which imposed high tariffs on imported grain, were repealed in 1846, signaling the beginning of a new era in trade policy. The subsequent proliferation of free trade agreements, such as the Cobden-Chevalier Treaty between Britain and France, exemplified the move towards reducing trade barriers and promoting international commerce. These agreements fostered economic growth and paved the way for the establishment of a more integrated global economy.

The 20th century witnessed the emergence of multilateral trade institutions, with the General Agreement on Tariffs and Trade (GATT) being a cornerstone of the post-World War II economic order. Established in 1947, GATT aimed to promote international trade by reducing tariffs and eliminating trade barriers. The principles of non-discrimination and reciprocity underpinned its framework, fostering a more open and rules-based trading system. The transformation of GATT into the World Trade Organization (WTO) in 1995 further institutionalized these principles, providing a forum for resolving trade disputes and negotiating trade agreements.

In recent decades, the rise of regional trade blocs has reshaped the landscape of global trade. The European Union (EU), the North American Free Trade Agreement (NAFTA), and the Asia-Pacific Economic Cooperation (APEC) are notable examples of regional integration initiatives that have facilitated cross-border trade and investment. These blocs aim to harmonize regulations, reduce trade barriers, and create larger markets for businesses. However, they also raise concerns about trade diversion and the potential marginalization of countries outside these agreements.

Understanding the evolution of global trade policies is crucial for businesses operating in the international arena. By analyzing historical trends and contemporary developments, companies can better navigate the complexities of trade regulations, identify opportunities for growth, and anticipate the impact of political changes on their operations. This chapter provides a comprehensive overview of how trade policies have shaped the global business landscape, offering valuable insights for businesses seeking to thrive

CHAPTER 2: THE EVOLUTION OF GLOBAL TRADE POLICIES

in an interconnected world.

3

Chapter 3: The Role of Government Regulations

Government regulations play a crucial role in shaping the business environment. Whether it's labor laws, environmental policies, or antitrust regulations, governments influence how companies operate and compete. This chapter investigates the rationale behind various regulations and their impact on different industries. Case studies of significant regulatory changes, such as the introduction of the Sarbanes-Oxley Act in the United States or the European Union's General Data Protection Regulation (GDPR), illustrate how political decisions can transform business practices and affect global markets.

Labor laws are among the most fundamental regulations affecting businesses. They establish minimum standards for wages, working conditions, and employee rights, aiming to protect workers from exploitation and ensure fair treatment. For instance, the introduction of the Fair Labor Standards Act (FLSA) in the United States in 1938 set a precedent for regulating working hours, minimum wage, and child labor. These regulations have since evolved to address new challenges, such as gig economy work and remote employment, reflecting changing societal values and economic conditions.

Environmental policies are another critical area of government regulation, addressing the impact of business activities on the natural world. Regulations such as the Clean Air Act and the Clean Water Act in the United States set stringent standards for pollution control, requiring companies to adopt sustainable practices and invest in green technologies. The European Union's Emissions Trading System (ETS) is a notable example of a market-based approach to reducing greenhouse gas emissions, encouraging businesses to innovate and reduce their carbon footprint. These regulations not only protect the environment but also create opportunities for businesses to develop new products and services in the green economy.

Antitrust regulations aim to promote competition and prevent monopolistic practices that can harm consumers and stifle innovation. The landmark antitrust case against Microsoft in the late 1990s, for example, demonstrated the government's commitment to curbing anti-competitive behavior in the tech industry. The case resulted in significant changes to Microsoft's business practices, fostering a more competitive and dynamic software market. Similarly, recent scrutiny of tech giants like Google, Amazon, and Facebook highlights the ongoing relevance of antitrust regulations in addressing the challenges of the digital age.

The introduction of the Sarbanes-Oxley Act (SOX) in 2002 marked a significant regulatory shift in the United States, following corporate scandals such as Enron and WorldCom. SOX aimed to enhance corporate governance, improve financial transparency, and restore investor confidence. Key provisions included stricter requirements for financial reporting, increased accountability for corporate executives, and the establishment of the Public Company Accounting Oversight Board (PCAOB) to oversee audits. The act's implementation had a profound impact on businesses, leading to increased compliance costs and changes in corporate governance practices.

The European Union's General Data Protection Regulation (GDPR), implemented in 2018, represents one of the most comprehensive data protection frameworks in the world. GDPR establishes strict guidelines for the collection, processing, and storage of personal data, aiming to protect individuals' privacy rights. Its extraterritorial scope means that businesses operating in or targeting EU citizens must comply with its provisions, regardless of their location. The regulation has prompted companies to adopt robust data protection measures, enhancing consumer trust and setting a global benchmark for privacy standards.

Understanding the role of government regulations is essential for businesses to navigate the complex and dynamic regulatory landscape. By examining the rationale behind regulations and their impact on different industries, companies can develop strategies to ensure compliance, mitigate risks, and seize opportunities for innovation. This chapter provides valuable insights into how political decisions shape the business environment, highlighting the importance of regulatory awareness and adaptability in achieving long-term success.

4

Chapter 4: Political Risk and Business Strategy

Operating in multiple countries exposes businesses to a myriad of political risks, ranging from government instability to expropriation of assets. Identifying and managing these risks is essential for multinational corporations. This chapter explores the concept of political risk, its sources, and the strategies businesses employ to mitigate its impact. Through real-world examples, we examine how companies assess political environments, build contingency plans, and make strategic decisions to safeguard their interests. By understanding political risk, businesses can better navigate the uncertainties of the global marketplace.

Political risk can manifest in various forms, including changes in government policies, regulatory shifts, civil unrest, and geopolitical tensions. For example, the nationalization of the oil industry in Venezuela in the early 2000s posed significant challenges for foreign oil companies operating in the country. The expropriation of assets and renegotiation of contracts disrupted business operations and led to substantial financial losses. Such instances highlight the importance of understanding the political landscape and anticipating potential risks to protect investments.

One approach to managing political risk is through comprehensive risk assessment and due diligence. Businesses can analyze the political stability, regulatory environment, and potential for social unrest in target markets to make informed decisions. For instance, before entering a new market, companies can conduct scenario analysis to evaluate the potential impact of different political developments on their operations. By identifying key risk factors and assessing their likelihood and severity, businesses can develop strategies to mitigate their impact.

Another strategy for managing political risk is diversification. By operating in multiple countries and regions, businesses can spread their risk and reduce their exposure to any single political event. For example, multinational corporations like Nestlé and Procter & Gamble have diversified their operations across various markets, enabling them to offset losses in one region with gains in another. Diversification also allows companies to capitalize on growth opportunities in emerging markets while minimizing the impact of political instability in any one country.

Building strong relationships with local stakeholders is also crucial for managing political risk. Companies can engage with government officials, community leaders, and non-governmental organizations to foster goodwill and build trust. For instance, mining companies operating in politically sensitive regions often collaborate with local communities to address social and environmental concerns. By demonstrating a commitment to corporate social responsibility and sustainable development, businesses can mitigate the risk of opposition and gain support from local stakeholders.

In some cases, businesses may choose to transfer political risk through insurance or financial instruments. Political risk insurance, offered by organizations such as the Multilateral Investment Guarantee Agency (MIGA) and private insurers, can provide coverage against risks such as expropriation, political violence, and currency inconvertibility. Additionally, companies can use financial derivatives, such as currency swaps and options, to hedge against exchange rate fluctuations resulting from political instability.

Understanding and managing political risk is essential for businesses to thrive in the global marketplace. By adopting a proactive and strategic approach, companies can navigate the complexities of political environments, protect their investments, and seize opportunities for growth. This chapter provides valuable insights into the sources of political risk and the strategies businesses can employ to mitigate its impact, offering practical guidance for navigating the uncertainties of the global business landscape.

5

Chapter 5: Societal Values and Corporate Responsibility

Societal values and expectations profoundly influence business practices. As societies evolve, so do the demands for corporate responsibility and ethical conduct. This chapter examines the growing importance of corporate social responsibility (CSR) and the role of businesses in addressing social issues. From environmental sustainability to fair labor practices, companies are increasingly held accountable for their impact on society. Through case studies of successful CSR initiatives, we explore how businesses can align their strategies with societal values, enhancing their reputation and fostering long-term success.

Corporate social responsibility has become a key component of business strategy in the 21st century. Companies are no longer solely judged by their financial performance but also by their contributions to social and environmental causes. The shift towards CSR is driven by changing societal values, increased awareness of global challenges, and the growing influence of stakeholders such as customers, employees, and investors. Businesses that embrace CSR can build stronger relationships with their stakeholders, enhance their brand reputation, and create long-term value.

One example of successful CSR is the environmental sustainability initiatives undertaken by Unilever, a global consumer goods company. Unilever's

CHAPTER 5: SOCIETAL VALUES AND CORPORATE RESPONSIBILITY

Sustainable Living Plan, launched in 2010, aims to reduce the company's environmental footprint, improve health and well-being, and enhance livelihoods across its value chain. The plan includes ambitious targets such as halving the environmental impact of its products, sourcing 100% of agricultural raw materials sustainably, and improving the health and well-being of one billion people. By integrating sustainability into its business strategy, Unilever has not only reduced its environmental impact but also gained a competitive advantage and strengthened its relationships with consumers and stakeholders.

Fair labor practices are another critical aspect of corporate responsibility. Companies are increasingly expected to ensure fair wages, safe working conditions, and respect for workers' rights throughout their supply chains. The apparel industry, in particular, has faced scrutiny over labor practices in factories located in developing countries. Brands like Patagonia and Fair Trade USA have taken significant steps to address these concerns by implementing fair labor standards, conducting regular audits, and promoting transparency in their supply chains. These efforts demonstrate that ethical labor practices can coexist with business success, fostering trust and loyalty among consumers.

Corporate philanthropy and community engagement are also important elements of CSR. Companies can make meaningful contributions to society by supporting education, healthcare, and social initiatives in the communities where they operate. For instance, Microsoft's philanthropic efforts focus on empowering individuals and organizations through technology, education, and workforce development. Through initiatives like the Microsoft AI for Good program and the Microsoft Philanthropies division, the company has made significant strides in addressing social challenges and promoting inclusive growth.

The rise of socially responsible investing (SRI) further underscores the importance of CSR in the business world. Investors are increasingly considering environmental, social, and governance (ESG) factors when making investment decisions. ESG criteria assess a company's performance in areas such as environmental sustainability, social responsibility, and corporate governance. Companies that excel in these areas are more likely to attract investment and enjoy long-term financial success. By aligning their strategies with societal values, businesses can meet the expectations of socially conscious investors and create value for all stakeholders.

Understanding the significance of corporate social responsibility is essential for businesses to thrive in today's society. By embracing ethical practices, addressing social and environmental challenges, and engaging with stakeholders, companies can build a positive reputation, foster trust, and contribute to a more sustainable and inclusive world. This chapter provides valuable insights into the evolving expectations of corporate responsibility and the strategies businesses can adopt to align with societal values, driving long-term success and positive impact.

6

Chapter 6: The Influence of Political Lobbying

Lobbying has long been a powerful tool for businesses to influence political decisions and shape policies to their advantage. This chapter delves into the world of political lobbying, exploring its mechanisms, strategies, and ethical considerations. By analyzing notable lobbying efforts and their outcomes, we gain insights into how businesses advocate for their interests and navigate the political landscape. Additionally, we examine the controversies surrounding lobbying, such as the potential for undue influence and the need for transparency in the political process.

Political lobbying involves various activities, such as meeting with legislators, funding political campaigns, and organizing grassroots movements to advocate for specific policies. Businesses often employ professional lobbyists who have expertise in the legislative process and established relationships with policymakers. These lobbyists work to influence legislation, regulations, and government decisions in ways that benefit their clients.

One prominent example of political lobbying is the pharmaceutical industry's efforts to influence healthcare policy in the United States. Pharmaceutical companies invest significant resources in lobbying to shape drug pricing, intellectual property rights, and regulatory approvals. For instance, during the passage of the Affordable Care Act (ACA) in 2010, the pharmaceutical industry played a crucial role in negotiating provisions related to drug pricing and market access. By leveraging their lobbying power, pharmaceutical companies aim to protect their interests and ensure favorable policy outcomes.

The technology industry is another sector where lobbying efforts are prominent. Companies like Google, Facebook, and Apple engage in extensive lobbying to influence policies on data privacy, antitrust regulations, and digital commerce. These tech giants advocate for policies that promote innovation and competition while addressing concerns related to data protection and market dominance. The debates over net neutrality and the regulation of digital platforms highlight the significant impact of lobbying on the technology sector.

While lobbying can be a legitimate way for businesses to advocate for their interests, it also raises ethical concerns. The potential for undue influence, conflicts of interest, and lack of transparency can undermine public trust in the political process. High-profile cases, such as the lobbying scandal involving Jack Abramoff in the early 2000s, have exposed the darker side of lobbying and led to calls for reform. Efforts to address these concerns include implementing stricter lobbying disclosure requirements, establishing ethics committees, and promoting transparency in political contributions.

Despite the controversies, lobbying remains an essential tool for businesses to navigate the political landscape. Effective lobbying requires a deep understanding of the legislative process, building relationships with policymakers, and crafting persuasive arguments. Businesses that engage in lobbying must also consider the ethical implications of their actions and strive to balance their interests with the public good.

Understanding the influence of political lobbying is crucial for businesses operating in regulated industries. By examining the mechanisms and strategies of lobbying, companies can better advocate for their interests, navigate the complexities of the political landscape, and contribute to informed policymaking. This chapter provides valuable insights into the world of political lobbying, highlighting its significance, ethical considerations, and impact on business practices and public policy.

7

Chapter 7: The Impact of Geopolitical Conflicts

Geopolitical conflicts can have far-reaching consequences for global business operations. Wars, territorial disputes, and diplomatic tensions create uncertainties that affect trade, investment, and supply chains. This chapter explores the impact of geopolitical conflicts on businesses, using historical and contemporary examples. We analyze how companies adapt to changing geopolitical landscapes, build resilience, and engage in crisis management. Understanding the interplay between geopolitics and business is crucial for companies operating in regions prone to conflict.

Geopolitical conflicts often disrupt trade routes and supply chains, leading to increased costs and delays for businesses. The Suez Canal crisis of 1956, for example, temporarily halted one of the world's most important maritime trade routes, affecting global shipping and trade. More recently, the ongoing tensions between the United States and China have led to trade disputes, tariffs, and supply chain disruptions. Businesses that rely on global supply chains must navigate these challenges by diversifying suppliers, building inventory buffers, and developing contingency plans.

Investment decisions are also influenced by geopolitical conflicts. Political instability and conflict can deter foreign investment and create uncertainty for businesses. The Russian annexation of Crimea in 2014, for instance, led to economic sanctions and a decline in foreign investment in Russia. Companies operating in conflict-prone regions must carefully assess the risks and potential impact on their investments. Strategies such as political risk insurance, joint ventures with local partners, and engaging in corporate diplomacy can help mitigate these risks.

Geopolitical conflicts also affect the labor market and workforce mobility. Conflicts often lead to displacement and migration, creating challenges for businesses in terms of labor availability and talent retention. The Syrian refugee crisis, for example, has had significant implications for labor markets in neighboring countries and beyond. Businesses must adapt to these changes by developing flexible workforce strategies, investing in training and development programs, and supporting the integration of displaced workers.

Building resilience to geopolitical conflicts requires a proactive approach to crisis management and risk mitigation. Companies can develop crisis management plans that outline response strategies, communication protocols, and recovery measures. For example, during the COVID-19 pandemic, businesses implemented crisis management plans to address supply chain disruptions, protect employee health, and adapt to changing market conditions. By building resilience and agility, companies can better navigate the uncertainties of geopolitical conflicts and ensure business continuity.

Engaging in corporate diplomacy is another strategy for managing geopolitical risks. Corporate diplomacy involves building relationships with governments, international organizations, and other stakeholders to advocate for favorable policies and address geopolitical challenges. Companies like ExxonMobil and Boeing have long engaged in corporate diplomacy to navigate complex geopolitical environments and protect their interests. By fostering dialogue and collaboration, businesses can contribute to conflict resolution and promote stability in the regions where they operate.

Understanding the impact of geopolitical conflicts is essential for businesses to thrive in a globalized world. By analyzing historical and contemporary examples, companies can develop strategies to navigate the complexities of geopolitical landscapes, build resilience, and ensure business continuity. This chapter provides valuable insights into the interplay between geopolitics and business, highlighting the importance of proactive risk management and corporate diplomacy in addressing geopolitical challenges.

8

Chapter 8: The Role of International Organizations

International organizations, such as the United Nations (UN), International Monetary Fund (IMF), and World Bank, play a significant role in shaping global business practices. This chapter examines the functions and influence of these organizations, focusing on their efforts to promote economic stability, development, and cooperation. Through case studies, we explore how international organizations address global challenges, such as poverty, inequality, and climate change, and how their policies impact businesses. Understanding the role of these institutions is essential for companies operating in the global marketplace.

The United Nations, established in 1945, is a central player in international diplomacy and global governance. Its various specialized agencies, such as the World Health Organization (WHO) and the United Nations Environment Programme (UNEP), work to address global issues ranging from health crises to environmental sustainability. For example, the UN's Sustainable Development Goals (SDGs) set ambitious targets for eradicating poverty, promoting education, and ensuring environmental sustainability by 2030. Businesses are encouraged to align their strategies with the SDGs, contributing to global development while enhancing their sustainability credentials.

The International Monetary Fund (IMF) is another key institution that influences global business practices. The IMF provides financial assistance and policy advice to countries facing economic challenges, promoting macroeconomic stability and growth. Through its lending programs and technical assistance, the IMF helps countries implement structural reforms, stabilize their economies, and improve their investment climate. For instance, during the European debt crisis, the IMF played a crucial role in supporting countries like Greece and Portugal, providing financial assistance and policy guidance to help them overcome their economic difficulties.

The World Bank, established in 1944, focuses on reducing poverty and promoting sustainable development. It provides financial and technical assistance to developing countries for projects that improve infrastructure, healthcare, education, and economic development. The World Bank's initiatives, such as the International Finance Corporation (IFC) and the Multilateral Investment Guarantee Agency (MIGA), support private sector investment and development. For example, the World Bank's support for renewable energy projects in developing countries has helped expand access to clean energy, reduce greenhouse gas emissions, and create economic opportunities.

Regional organizations, such as the European Union (EU) and the Association of Southeast Asian Nations (ASEAN), also play a significant role in shaping business practices within their regions. The EU, with its single market and common regulatory framework, promotes economic integration and facilitates cross-border trade and investment among its member states. Similarly, ASEAN aims to create a single market and production base, enhancing economic cooperation and competitiveness in Southeast Asia. Businesses operating in these regions benefit from harmonized regulations, reduced trade barriers, and increased market access.

International organizations also address global challenges that impact businesses, such as climate change and social inequality. The Paris Agreement, adopted under the United Nations Framework Convention on Climate Change (UNFCCC), aims to limit global warming to well below 2 degrees Celsius above pre-industrial levels. Businesses are encouraged to adopt sustainable practices and reduce their carbon footprint in line with the agreement's goals. Similarly, initiatives like the World Bank's Human Capital Project emphasize the importance of investing in education, healthcare, and skills development to enhance productivity and economic growth.

Understanding the role of international organizations is essential for businesses to navigate the complexities of the global marketplace. By engaging with these institutions and aligning their strategies with global goals, companies can contribute to sustainable development, enhance their reputation, and access new markets and opportunities. This chapter provides valuable insights into the influence of international organizations on global business practices, highlighting the importance of collaboration and multilateralism in addressing global challenges.

9

Chapter 9: The Power of Public Opinion

Public opinion can be a formidable force in shaping business practices and political decisions. In an era of social media and instant communication, public sentiment can rapidly influence corporate reputations and government policies. This chapter investigates the dynamics of public opinion, exploring how businesses respond to societal pressures and manage their public image. We analyze case studies of companies that faced public backlash or gained public support, highlighting the importance of effective communication and stakeholder engagement in navigating the complex interplay between public opinion, politics, and business.

The rise of social media has amplified the power of public opinion, enabling individuals and communities to voice their concerns and mobilize around social issues. Companies must be attuned to public sentiment and responsive to societal expectations to maintain their reputations and build trust with stakeholders. For example, the backlash against Nike's use of sweatshop labor in the 1990s prompted the company to implement significant changes in its labor practices and supply chain management. Nike's efforts to address public concerns and improve transparency helped restore its reputation and regain consumer trust.

Public opinion can also shape government policies and regulatory decisions. Activism and advocacy by civil society groups, consumers, and employees can influence policymakers and drive legislative changes. The environmental movement, for instance, has played a critical role in advancing policies on climate change, renewable energy, and pollution control. Companies that align their strategies with public concerns and advocate for positive change can build stronger relationships with stakeholders and contribute to sustainable development.

Managing public opinion requires effective communication and engagement with stakeholders. Companies must be transparent, authentic, and proactive in addressing societal issues. For instance, Patagonia, an outdoor apparel company, has built a strong reputation for its commitment to environmental sustainability and social responsibility. Through initiatives like the "1% for the Planet" pledge and campaigns to protect public lands, Patagonia has engaged consumers, employees, and communities in its mission to protect the environment. By aligning its business practices with public values, Patagonia has cultivated a loyal customer base and enhanced its brand reputation.

Public opinion can also influence corporate governance and decision-making. Shareholder activism, for example, involves investors advocating for changes in corporate policies and practices to address social, environmental, and governance issues. Activist shareholders can use their voting power to influence board decisions, propose resolutions, and push for greater accountability and transparency. High-profile cases, such as the campaigns led by activist investor Carl Icahn, demonstrate the impact of shareholder activism on corporate governance and business strategies.

In addition to external pressures, companies must also consider the opinions and values of their internal stakeholders, such as employees. Employee activism and advocacy can drive corporate change and shape business practices. For example, employee protests at major tech companies like Google and Amazon have highlighted issues such as workplace diversity, ethical AI development, and labor rights. Companies that listen to and address employee concerns can foster a positive work environment, enhance employee engagement, and attract top talent.

Understanding the power of public opinion is essential for businesses to navigate the complexities of the modern marketplace. By being responsive to societal pressures, engaging with stakeholders, and aligning their practices with public values, companies can build trust, enhance their reputation, and contribute to positive social change. This chapter provides valuable insights into the dynamics of public opinion and its impact on business practices and political decisions, highlighting the importance of effective communication and stakeholder engagement in achieving long-term success.

10

Chapter 10: The Challenges of Global Governance

Global governance is essential for addressing transnational challenges that affect businesses and societies alike. From climate change to cybersecurity, complex issues require coordinated efforts and international cooperation. This chapter explores the challenges and opportunities of global governance, examining the role of multinational corporations, governments, and international organizations in finding solutions. By analyzing case studies of successful global initiatives, we gain insights into how businesses can contribute to global governance and navigate the intricate web of international regulations and standards.

Climate change is one of the most pressing global challenges, requiring coordinated action from governments, businesses, and international organizations. The Paris Agreement, adopted in 2015, represents a landmark effort to address climate change through international cooperation. The agreement sets targets for reducing greenhouse gas emissions and encourages countries to submit their own climate action plans. Businesses play a crucial role in achieving these targets by adopting sustainable practices, investing in renewable energy, and reducing their carbon footprint. Companies like Tesla and Ørsted have demonstrated leadership in the transition to a low-carbon economy, driving innovation and demonstrating the potential for sustainable

CHAPTER 10: THE CHALLENGES OF GLOBAL GOVERNANCE

business models.

Cybersecurity is another critical issue that demands global governance. The increasing interconnectedness of the digital world has created new vulnerabilities and risks for businesses and societies. International cooperation is essential for developing standards, sharing intelligence, and combating cyber threats. The European Union's General Data Protection Regulation (GDPR) sets a high standard for data protection and privacy, influencing global practices and raising awareness of cybersecurity issues. Companies must navigate a complex regulatory landscape, implement robust security measures, and collaborate with governments and other stakeholders to protect their digital assets and ensure data privacy.

Global health is another area where international cooperation and governance are essential. The COVID-19 pandemic highlighted the importance of coordinated efforts to address public health crises. Organizations like the World Health Organization (WHO) and the Coalition for Epidemic Preparedness Innovations (CEPI) played crucial roles in coordinating the global response, developing vaccines, and supporting healthcare systems. Businesses also contributed to the response by pivoting their operations to produce medical supplies, supporting research and development, and ensuring the safety of their employees and customers. The pandemic underscored the need for resilient healthcare systems, robust supply chains, and international solidarity in addressing global health challenges.

Trade and economic governance are also critical components of global governance. Institutions like the World Trade Organization (WTO) and the International Monetary Fund (IMF) facilitate international trade and economic stability. Trade agreements and economic policies set the rules for cross-border commerce, influencing business practices and market access. For example, the Trans-Pacific Partnership (TPP) aimed to create a comprehensive trade agreement among Pacific Rim countries, promoting economic integration and setting high standards for labor, environmental, and intellectual property protections. Although the TPP faced challenges, its principles continue to shape regional trade agreements and influence global trade policies.

Global governance also encompasses efforts to address social issues such as poverty, inequality, and human rights. Initiatives like the United Nations' Sustainable Development Goals (SDGs) provide a framework for countries, businesses, and civil society to collaborate on achieving common objectives. The private sector plays a vital role in advancing these goals by integrating sustainability into business strategies, investing in social and environmental initiatives, and fostering inclusive growth. Companies that embrace the SDGs can create shared value, enhance their reputation, and contribute to a more equitable and sustainable world.

Challenges in global governance often arise from competing interests, differing national priorities, and the complexity of coordinating actions across multiple stakeholders. Achieving consensus on global issues requires diplomacy, negotiation, and compromise. The Paris Agreement on climate change, for example, faced challenges in balancing the interests of developed and developing countries, ensuring fairness, and securing commitments from all parties. Despite these difficulties, the agreement represents a significant step forward in global climate governance, demonstrating the potential for international cooperation to address pressing global challenges.

Businesses operating in the global marketplace must navigate the intricate web of international regulations and standards. Compliance with these regulations is essential for accessing markets, avoiding legal risks, and maintaining a positive reputation. For example, multinational companies must adhere to anti-corruption laws such as the US Foreign Corrupt Practices Act (FCPA) and the UK Bribery Act, which prohibit bribery and corruption in international business transactions. By implementing robust compliance programs and fostering a culture of ethics and integrity, companies can mitigate legal risks and build trust with stakeholders.

The role of multinational corporations in global governance extends beyond compliance. Companies can actively participate in shaping international standards, contributing to policy discussions, and advocating for sustainable practices. For instance, the United Nations Global Compact provides a platform for businesses to commit to principles of human rights, labor standards, environmental sustainability, and anti-corruption. By joining the Global Compact, companies demonstrate their commitment to responsible business practices and collaborate with other stakeholders to advance global goals.

Understanding the challenges and opportunities of global governance is essential for businesses to thrive in an interconnected world. By engaging with international organizations, aligning their strategies with global goals, and navigating the complex regulatory landscape, companies can contribute to sustainable development and create long-term value. This chapter provides valuable insights into the dynamics of global governance, highlighting the importance of collaboration, compliance, and corporate responsibility in addressing transnational challenges.

11

Chapter 11: The Future of Work in a Changing World

The future of work is being shaped by technological advancements, demographic shifts, and evolving societal values. This chapter explores the implications of these changes for businesses and workers alike. From automation and artificial intelligence to remote work and gig economies, we examine how political decisions and societal trends influence the future of work. By analyzing emerging trends and their impact on industries, we provide insights into how businesses can adapt to the changing landscape and prepare for the workforce of the future.

Technological advancements, particularly in automation and artificial intelligence (AI), are transforming the nature of work. Robots and AI-powered systems are increasingly capable of performing tasks that were once the exclusive domain of human workers. While automation offers opportunities for increased efficiency and productivity, it also raises concerns about job displacement and the need for workforce reskilling. Governments and businesses must work together to address these challenges by investing in education, training, and upskilling programs to prepare workers for the jobs of the future.

Remote work and flexible work arrangements have gained prominence, accelerated by the COVID-19 pandemic. The shift to remote work has demonstrated the potential for increased productivity, reduced commuting time, and improved work-life balance. However, it also presents challenges related to employee engagement, collaboration, and mental health. Companies must adapt their management practices, invest in digital infrastructure, and create supportive work environments to ensure the success of remote and hybrid work models.

The gig economy, characterized by short-term contracts and freelance work, is reshaping the traditional employment landscape. Platforms like Uber, Airbnb, and Upwork have created new opportunities for flexible work, enabling individuals to monetize their skills and assets. However, gig workers often lack the benefits and protections associated with traditional employment, such as health insurance, retirement plans, and job security. Policymakers and businesses must find ways to balance flexibility with security, ensuring fair treatment and protection for gig workers.

Demographic shifts, such as aging populations and changing workforce demographics, also influence the future of work. In many countries, aging populations pose challenges related to labor shortages, increased healthcare costs, and the need for pension reforms. Businesses must adapt to these changes by promoting diversity and inclusion, implementing age-friendly practices, and leveraging the skills and experience of older workers. At the same time, the entry of younger generations into the workforce brings new perspectives, digital skills, and demands for purpose-driven work.

Evolving societal values, such as the emphasis on work-life balance, mental health, and sustainability, are shaping the expectations of workers and consumers alike. Companies that prioritize employee well-being, foster inclusive cultures, and adopt sustainable practices are more likely to attract and retain talent. For example, companies like Salesforce and Unilever have implemented initiatives to support employee well-being, promote diversity and inclusion, and reduce their environmental impact. By aligning with societal values, businesses can create a positive work environment, enhance their reputation, and drive long-term success.

Understanding the future of work and its implications is essential for businesses to navigate the changing landscape and remain competitive. By embracing technological advancements, adapting to new work models, and addressing the needs and expectations of a diverse workforce, companies can build resilient and agile organizations. This chapter provides valuable insights into the trends shaping the future of work, offering strategies for businesses to thrive in a dynamic and evolving world.

12

Chapter 12: Navigating the Marketplace of Ideas

In the ever-evolving marketplace of ideas, businesses must navigate a complex landscape of political, societal, and economic influences. This chapter synthesizes the key themes explored throughout the book, offering strategies for businesses to thrive in this dynamic environment. We emphasize the importance of adaptability, innovation, and ethical conduct in navigating the interplay between politics and society. By understanding the forces shaping global business, companies can seize opportunities, mitigate risks, and contribute to a more sustainable and inclusive global economy.

Adaptability is a crucial attribute for businesses operating in a rapidly changing world. The ability to anticipate and respond to shifts in political landscapes, regulatory environments, and societal values is essential for long-term success. Companies that foster a culture of innovation and agility can better navigate uncertainties and capitalize on emerging opportunities. For example, tech companies like Google and Amazon continuously innovate and adapt their business models to stay ahead in a competitive market. By embracing change and fostering a growth mindset, businesses can remain resilient and thrive in the face of challenges.

Innovation is another key driver of success in the marketplace of ideas. Companies that invest in research and development, embrace new technologies, and explore creative solutions can differentiate themselves and create value for their stakeholders. For instance, Tesla's commitment to innovation in electric vehicles and renewable energy has positioned the company as a leader in the transition to a sustainable future. By fostering a culture of innovation, businesses can drive progress, address global challenges, and unlock new growth opportunities.

Ethical conduct and corporate responsibility are essential components of sustainable business practices. Companies that prioritize transparency, integrity, and social responsibility can build trust with stakeholders and enhance their reputation. Ethical behavior extends beyond compliance with regulations; it involves aligning business practices with societal values and addressing the impact of corporate actions on people and the planet. Businesses that demonstrate a commitment to ethical conduct, such as Patagonia's dedication to environmental sustainability and social justice, can inspire loyalty and support from consumers, employees, and investors.

Collaboration is also vital for navigating the marketplace of ideas. By engaging with governments, international organizations, civil society, and other stakeholders, businesses can contribute to informed policy-making, address global challenges, and promote sustainable development. Public-private partnerships, industry coalitions, and multi-stakeholder initiatives provide platforms for collaboration and collective action. For example, the World Economic Forum's Platform for Shaping the Future of Global Public Goods brings together businesses, governments, and civil society to address pressing global issues such as climate change, health, and digital transformation. By fostering collaboration, businesses can amplify their impact and drive positive change.

Understanding the forces shaping global business is essential for companies to thrive in the marketplace of ideas. By synthesizing insights from politics, society, and economics, businesses can develop strategies to navigate complex environments, mitigate risks, and seize opportunities. This chapter provides a comprehensive framework for navigating the interplay between politics and society, offering practical guidance for businesses to contribute to a more sustainable and inclusive global economy.

CHAPTER 12: NAVIGATING THE MARKETPLACE OF IDEAS

Book Description:

In "The Marketplace of Ideas: How Politics and Society Shape Global Business," discover the intricate dance between politics, society, and commerce that shapes the global economy. This insightful book delves deep into how political systems, societal values, and international relations influence business practices, trade policies, and corporate strategies.

Each chapter unpacks a vital aspect of this dynamic relationship, from the historical evolution of trade policies and the role of government regulations to the impact of geopolitical conflicts and the power of public opinion. Through real-world examples and case studies, the book offers a comprehensive understanding of the challenges and opportunities businesses face in an interconnected world.

Explore how multinational corporations navigate political risks, engage in lobbying efforts, and adapt to societal expectations of corporate responsibility. Learn about the influence of international organizations, the future of work shaped by technological advancements and demographic shifts, and the essential role of global governance in addressing transnational challenges like climate change and cybersecurity.

"The Marketplace of Ideas" provides practical insights and strategies for businesses to thrive in a complex global landscape. By embracing adaptability, innovation, and ethical conduct, companies can seize opportunities, mitigate risks, and contribute to a more sustainable and inclusive global economy.

Perfect for business leaders, policymakers, and anyone interested in the interplay between politics, society, and commerce, this book is a must-read for understanding the forces that shape our world.

www.ingramcontent.com/pod-product-compliance
Lightning Source LLC
LaVergne TN
LVHW020459080526
838202LV00057B/6043